A Quiz Book of the Victorian Era

Christina Croft

Contents

Inventors & Inventions 5

Assassinations & Attempted Assassinations 6

Authors 7

Poets 8

Composers 9

Artists........................10

Murders & Murderers 11

Buildings & Monuments 12

Politicians & Statesmen 13

Who Lived Here?........................14

Queen Victoria 15

Other Monarchs of the Victorian Era 16

Tragedies and Accidents 17

Business & Retail........................18

Battles & Warfare 19

Scandals 20

Reformers & Philanthropists 21

Popular Songs 22

Sports, Games & Leisure........................23

Medicine & Health 24

Explorers 25

Answers to Inventors & Inventions 26

Answers to Assassinations & Attempted
Assassinations 27

Answers to Authors........................28

Answers to Poets........................29

Answers to Composers........................30

Answers to Artists...31

Answers to Murders & Murderers................................32

Answers to Buildings & Monuments...........................33

Answers to Politicians & Statesmen 34

Answers to Who Lived Here?.......................................35

Answers to Queen Victoria...36

Answers to Other Monarchs of the Victorian Era 37

Answers to Tragedies and Accidents...........................38

Answers to Business & Retail.......................................39

Answers to Battles & Warfare 40

Answers to Scandals..41

Answers to Reformers & Philanthropists 42

Answers to Popular Songs 43

Answers to Sports, Games & Leisure..........................44

Answers to Medicine & Health 45

Answers to Explorers 46

Inventors & Inventions

1. Which invention was used for the first time at a football match in Sheffield in 1878?

2. Which British town was the first to use electric trams in 1885?

3. Which bicycle was first introduced to Britain in 1879?

4. In 1860, which Frenchman patented the first internal combustion engine?

5. In what year was the first Zeppelin built?

6. Who invented the telephone?

7. Which inventor of the telegraph gave his name to a telegraph code?

8. Which American invented vulcanised rubber in 1839?

9. Who, in 1849, invented the safety pin?

10. Which popular drink was first created by James Pemberton in 1886?

Answers on Page 26

Assassinations & Attempted Assassinations

1. For what was the aptly named Robert Pate arrested in 1850?

2. Which member of Queen Victoria's family was shot at in Brussels by a youth named Sipido?

3. Which President of France was shot and killed by an anarchist in 1894?

4. Which Chief Secretary for Ireland was assassinated during the Phoenix Park murders only hours after his arrival in Dublin?

5. Which King was killed by Gaetano Bresci in 1900?

6. Which Tsar of Russia was murdered by anarchists in 1881?

7. Whom did Giovanni Passannante attempt to assassinate in 1878?

8. Who killed Empress Elizabeth of Austria-Hungary in 1898?

9. Which American President was killed by Charles J. Guiteau?

10. Whom did Ferdinand Cohen-Blind attempt to assassinate in 1866 because he opposed the Austro-Prussian War?

Answers on Page 27

Authors

1. Which of the Bronte sisters died in Scarborough in 1849?

2. Which author had a canary named Dick?

3. Which author's real name was Mary Ann Evans?

4. Which British author was the son of a stonemason, and trained as an architect?

5. Which author, daughter of William Godwin and Mary Wollstonecraft, eloped with her poet lover to Italy at the age of sixteen?

6. Which author invented the pillar box?

7. Who wrote *The Time Machine*?

8. Which author was once assistant editor of the *Civil & Military Gazette* in Lahore?

9. Which two novels by Robert Louis Stevenson were published in 1886?

10. Who wrote *John Halifax, Gentleman*?

Answers on Page 28

Poets

1. Which poet had a dog named Flush, to whom she dedicated a poem?

2. What was the name of Dante Gabriel Rossetti's poet sister?

3. Which poem by Tennyson brought Queen Victoria 'the greatest comfort next to the Bible' following the death of Prince Albert?

4. Whose first collection of poetry was entitled *A Boy's Will*?

5. Who was the Poet Laureate when Queen Victoria ascended the throne in 1837?

6. Which poet was the son of the Headmaster of Rugby School?

7. Which poet was renowned for his limericks?

8. Which poet converted to Roman Catholicism in 1866 and became a Jesuit priest?

9. Which poet, who once believed himself to be Lord Byron, spent the greater part of his life in a lunatic asylum?

10. Which poet was at the centre of a scandal due to her alleged affair with Lord Melbourne?

Answers on Page 29

Composers

1. With whom did Arthur Sullivan collaborate on fourteen light operas?

2. Which composer set Newman's poem *The Dream of Gerontius* to music?

3. Who composed the music for Blake's poem *Jerusalem*?

4. Under what pseudonym did Michael Maybrick gain recognition for his compositions – notably *The Holy City*?

5. Which German composer, having been a guest of Queen Victoria and Prince Albert, remarked that, 'the only really nice, comfortable house in England... where one feels completely at home, is Buckingham Palace.'?

6. Which composer became the idol of King Ludwig II of Bavaria?

7. Which Russian composer's death was allegedly due to his contracting cholera by drinking contaminated water in 1893?

8. Who composed 'the 'Alice Polka' for Queen Victoria's second daughter?

9. In which Puccini opera is *Nessun Dorma* performed?

10. Which King of Hanover was largely responsible for Hector Berlioz' popularity in Germany?

Answers on Page 30

Artists

1. Which illustrator and author created Peter Rabbit and Jemima Puddleduck?

2. Who painted *The Fighting Temeraire*?

3. Which renowned painter created the lion sculptures in Trafalgar Square?

4. Which artistic brotherhood was founded by William Holman Hunt, John Everett Millais and Dante Gabriel Rossetti in 1848?

5. Which Northumbrian heroine did William Bell Scott portray in a dramatic painting?

6. Who created the statue of Queen Victoria, which stands outside Kensington Palace?

7. With which other artist was Van Gogh sharing a house when he cut off his own ear?

8. Who sculpted *The Burghers of Calais,* now situated in Victoria Tower Gardens in London?

9. Which landscape artist was born in Leeds in 1836?

10. Which German painter was known for his portraits of royalty including *Empress Eugenie Surrounded by her Ladies in Waiting*?

Answers on Page 31

Murders & Murderers

1. Which infamous murderer of three of her husbands is sometimes called Britain's first serial killer?

2. Who was accused of poisoning her husband, Charles, at *The Priory* in Balham in 1876?

3. Who is generally accepted as Jack the Ripper's last victim?

4. Who was known as the Rugeley Poisoner?

5. Which notorious baby farmer was hanged at Newgate in 1896?

6. Which Liverpool businessman was allegedly murdered by his American wife, Florence, in 1889?

7. Who, in 1892, allegedly 'took an axe and gave her mother forty whacks'?

8. Who was the first person to be murdered on a British train?

9. What was the verdict of Madeleine Smith's trial for the murder of her lover, Emile L'Angelier?

10. Who was known as 'The Massachusetts Borgia'?

Answers on Page 32

Buildings & Monuments

1. Which building did Joseph Paxton create to house the Great Exhibition of 1851?

2. Which monument to a famous British Admiral was constructed between 1840 and 1843?

3. Which iconic Parisian landmark was created as the entrance to the World's Fair of 1889?

4. Who designed the House of Parliament?

5. Which architect worked with Prince Albert on the construction of Osborne House on the Isle of Wight?

6. In which American state is the Carson Mansion?

7. Which famous Yorkshire viaduct was designed by John Sydney Crossley, and opened in 1875

8. Which Manchester building was constructed between 1853 and 1856 on the site of the Peterloo Massacre?

9. Which bridge, spanning the Avon gorge, was opened in 1864?

10. In what decade was New York's Brooklyn Bridge completed?

Answers on Page 33

Politicians & Statesmen

1. Who was known as the Iron Chancellor?

2. Which political activist, who died in 1872, campaigned for the unification of Italy?

3. Which future British Prime Minister won his first parliamentary seat in Oldham in 1900?

4. Who became President of France in 1871, following the abdication of Napoleon III?

5. Which future American President served as the U.S. Minister to Britain between 1853 and 1856?

6. How many Prime Ministers served during the reign of Queen Victoria?

7. Which American politician was known as 'The Great Compromiser'?

8. Who was the first Prime Minister of Canada?

9. Who was Arthur Wellesley?

10. Who was the British Prime Minister of Cape Colony between 1890 and 1896?

Answers on Page 34

Who Lived Here?

1. Which British Prime Minister lived at Hughenden Manor?

2. Which poet lived in Dove Cottage?

3. Which aristocratic and political family owned Blenheim Palace?

4. Who lived at 48 Doughty Street between 1837 and 1839?

5. For which banking family was Mentmore Towers built between 1852 and 1854?

6. Who lived in the Parsonage in Haworth?

7. Which poet, who was killed in World War I, lived for a time in the Old Vicarage in Grantchester?

8. Which poet lived at Farringford House on the Isle of Wight?

9. Which French author lived on the Rue de Bruxelles in Paris from 1889 until his death in 1902?

10. On which of the Channel Islands is Hauteville House, once home to Victor Hugo?

Answers on Page 35

Queen Victoria

1. Who was Queen Victoria's father?

2. What relation – apart from wife – was Queen Victoria to Prince Albert?

3. How many children did Queen Victoria have?

4. In what year was Queen Victoria created Empress of India?

5. What breed of dog was Queen Victoria's beloved Dash?

6. Where was Queen Victoria born?

7. Where did Queen Victoria die?

8. What relation was Queen Victoria to Kaiser Wilhelm II?

9. Of whom did Queen Victoria say, 'he speaks to me as if I were a public meeting'?

10. Where is Queen Victoria buried?

Answers on Page 36

Other Monarchs of the Victorian Era

1. Which German Emperor reigned for only three months in 1888?

2. Who was the first King of the Belgians?

3. Which Spanish monarch was king from the moment of his birth?

4. Who was the first German Emperor, following unification in 1871?

5. Which European monarch, who ascended the throne in 1848, reigned for sixty-six years?

6. Which King of France fled to England in disguise during the 1848 revolution?

7. Who was Tsar of Russia during the Crimean War?

8. Which Bavarian King was alleged to have drowned himself and his doctor?

9. Where did Crown Prince Rudolf of Austria-Hungary allegedly kill himself and his mistress?

10. How old was Queen Wilhelmina when she succeeded to the throne of the Netherlands in 1890?

Answers on Page 37

Tragedies and Accidents

1. What tragedy on the Khodinka meadow marred the celebrations for the coronation of Tsar Nicholas II in 1896?

2. Which railway tragedy was commemorated in a poem by William McGonagall?

3. Which Pennsylvanian city was devastated by a flood in 1889?

4. In what year was the Great Fire of Chicago?

5. The failure of which crop led to the Great Irish Famine of the 1840s?

6. What was the name of the pleasure steamer which sank off Gravesend in 1878, killing six hundred people?

7. Which illness struck San Francisco in 1900, ultimately killing 113 people?

8. Which Russian palace was almost destroyed by a fire which burned for three days in December 1837?

9. What weather feature led to the deaths of approximately two hundred people and six thousand animals in southern England in March 1891?

10. Which British city flooded, killing over two hundred people, when Dale Dyke Dam collapsed in 1864?

Answers on Page 38

Business & Retail

1. Which famous British retail chain began life in Leeds Market as a penny bazaar?

2. Where was Rowland Macy's original store located?

3. Which London store was the first in Britain to stock tinned baked beans in 1886?

4. Which London store, situated on Tottenham Court Road, was famous for supplying furniture to royalty and the aristocracy, including the Tsarina of Russia, and King George V?

5. Which American retail magnate coined the phrase 'Only – shopping days till Christmas', while working as a junior partner in Marshall Field & Company?

6. Which department store introduced the first escalator to London in 1898?

7. In which decade was the first mail order catalogue published in the United States?

8. In which U.S. state was the Heinz company founded?

9. Which famous pharmacy chain began life in Nottingham in 1849?

10. Which Parisian fashion house owed much of its success to the French Empress Eugenie?

Answers on Page 39

Battles & Warfare

1. Which two countries were involved in the Seven Weeks War of 1866?

2. Which Emperor was forced to abdicate following his defeat at Sedan in the Franco-Prussian War?

3. During which battle did the Charge of the Light Brigade occur?

4. Which famous British General was killed at Khartoum in 1885?

5. Which battle of the American Civil War led to the largest number of casualties?

6. Who were the combatants in the Thirty Days' War of 1897?

7. During which war did the British gain victory at Rorke's Drift?

8. In which year did the First Boer War begin?

9. Which war involving the British East India Company was fought between 1839 and 1842?

10. Who was the German Chief of Staff during the Franco-Prussian War?

Answers on Page 40

Scandals

1. Which political scandal rocked France in 1894 and remained unresolved for twelve years?

2. Whose claim that the Prince of Wales had fathered her child led to her incarceration in a lunatic asylum?

3. In which Scarborough stately home did the Prince of Wales become involved in the Baccarat Scandal?

4. On which street was a male brothel raided in 1889, leading to rumours that Queen Victoria's grandson had been a client there?

5. Who caused a scandal by living with the artist Millais, after claiming that her husband, John Ruskin, had failed to consummate their marriage?

6. Whose painting *A Portrait of Madame X* caused a scandal in 1884?

7. Who was dismissed from his position as tutor at Thorp Green following allegations of an affair with Lydia Robinson?

8. Which celebrated author and playwright was put on trial for gross indecency in 1895?

9. Which United States President survived the scandal of having fathered the child of his mistress, Maria Halpin?

10. Who was the first United States President to be impeached?

Answers on Page 41

Reformers & Philanthropists

1. Which prison reformer showed King Frederick William IV of Prussia around Newgate Prison by in 1842?

2. Who was 'the lady with the lamp'?

3. Which female social reformer and former slave led an armed group of seven hundred slaves during the Combahee River Raid in the American Civil War?

4. Which social reformer campaigned for the repeal of the Contagious Diseases Act?

5. Which renowned chocolate manufacturer created the model village of Bourneville for his workers?

6. Who founded the Salvation Army?

7. Which pioneer of social housing published a series of articles entitled, 'Homes for the Poor'?

8. Which American banker established a model housing company for London's poor?

9. Which reforming Earl became Chairman of the London Ragged School Union in 1844?

10. Who was Sophia Louisa Jex-Blake?

Answers on Page 42

Popular Songs

1. Complete the title: *Father's a drunkard and mother is...*

2. What, according to a song by Arthur Sullivan & Adelaide Anne Proctor, might only be found by 'death's bright angel'?

3. Complete the title: *The man who broke the bank at....*

4. To which 'Dolly' was the soldier saying goodbye in the popular Boer War anthem?

5. Whom did Alfred, Lord Tennyson and Arthur Somervell invite into the garden?

6. What, according to Arthur French and George Persley, do 'many, sad and weary' cry 'every night so dreary'?

7. What is the title of the song which contains the lines: *'Just a song at twilight, when the lights are low'*?

8. What did 'Claribel' beg her mother to take away?

9. Which popular song was adopted as the anthem of the Royal Marines in 1889?

10. Where, according to the popular song with lyrics by Rudyard Kipling, do the 'flyin' fishes play'?

Answers on Page 43

Sports, Games & Leisure

1. Whose horse, *Persimmon,* won the 1897 Derby?

2. What was a diabolo?

3. Which team won the first F.A. tournament in 1871?

4. Which Marquis gave his name to the twelve rules set out for boxing matches in 1867?

5. For what did Spencer Gore gain fame in 1877?

6. Who was the first winner of the Ladies' Singles Championship at Wimbledon?

7. Who, in 1875, was the first man to swim the English Channel?

8. What sort of a race was held for the first time in Paris in 1868?

9. What was staged for the first time in Athens in 1896?

10. For what sort of entertainment was George Sangar famous?

Answers on Page 44

Medicine & Health

1. Who introduced antiseptic surgery to Britain?

2. Who first developed a vaccine against rabies?

3. Which Jamaican nurse was refused permission to travel with Florence Nightingale's nurses to the Crimea, so made her own way there and established her own hospital for the wounded?

4. At which London hospital did Florence Nightingale establish a training school for nurses?

5. What did Dr John Snow identify as the cause of the Soho cholera epidemic of 1854?

6. Who is known as the 'father of modern medicine'?

7. Who, in 1853, published his *Anatomy,* a text book which is still used by medical students today?

8. Who was the first woman to qualify as a physician in England?

9. What was unusual about Dr James Miranda Barry?

10. Which Scottish-Canadian doctor was hanged in 1892 for multiple murders?

Answers on Page 45

Explorers

1. Which British explorer was the first to have the Kama Sutra translated into English?

2. Who accompanied Robert O'Hara Burke on his journey from the south to the north of Australia?

3. Which Swiss explorer disguised herself as a man to explore Arab society?

4. Which explorer was employed by King Leopold II of the Belgians to carry out his designs for the Congo?

5. Which female explorer wrote the book, 'West African Studies'?

6. Who was the first European to walk across Australia from east to west?

7. Which Yorkshire-born explorer became the first female Fellow of the Royal Geographical Society?

8. Who, in 1888, travelled around the world in seventy-two days?

9. Who was the first female European to attempt to cross the Sahara Desert?

10. Whom did the mountaineer and explorer Fanny Bullock marry in 1882?

Answers on Page 46

Answers to Inventors & Inventions

1. Electric floodlighting

2. Blackpool

3. Penny Farthing

4. Etienne Lenoir

5. 1900

6. Alexander Graham Bell

7. Samuel Morse

8. Charles Goodyear

9. Walter Hunt

10. Coca Cola

Answers to Assassinations & Attempted Assassinations

1. Striking Queen Victoria's head with a cane

2. The Prince of Wales, later Edward VII

3. Marie François Sadi Carnot

4. Lord Frederick Cavendish

5. King Umberto I of Italy

6. Alexander II

7. King Umberto I of Italy

8. Luigi Lucheni

9. James Garfield

10. Otto von Bismarck

Answers to Authors

1. Anne

2. Charles Dickens

3. George Eliot

4. Thomas Hardy

5. Mary Shelley

6. Anthony Trollope

7. H.G. Wells

8. Rudyard Kipling

9. The Strange Case of Dr Jeckyl and Mr Hyde; and Kidnapped

10. Dinah Craik

Answers to Poets

1. Elizabeth Barret Browning

2. Christina

3. In Memoriam

4. Robert Frost

5. Robert Southey

6. Matthew Arnold

7. Edward Lear

8. Gerard Manley Hopkins

9. John Clare

10. Caroline Norton

Answers to Composers

1. W.S. Gilbert

2. Edward Elgar

3. Hubert Parry

4. Stephen Adams

5. Felix Mendelssohn

6. Richard Wagner

7. Pyotr Ilych Tchaikovsky

8. Johann Strauss

9. Turandot

10. King George V of Hanover

Answers to Artists

1. Beatrix Potter

2. J.M.W. Turner

3. Edwin Landseer

4. The Pre-Raphaelite Brotherhood

5. Grace Darling

6. Her daughter, Princess Louise

7. Paul Gauguin

8. Auguste Rodin

9. John Atkinson Grimshaw

10. Franz Winterhalter

Answers to Murders & Murderers

1. Mary Ann Cotton

2. Florence Bravo

3. Mary Kelly

4. William Palmer

5. Amelia Dyer

6. James Maybrick

7. Lizzie Borden

8. Thomas Briggs

9. Not Proven

10. Sarah Jane Robinson

Answers to Buildings & Monuments

1. The Crystal Palace

2. Nelson's Column

3. Eiffel Tower

4. Charles Barry

5. Thomas Cubitt

6. California

7. Ribbleshead Viaduct

8. Free Trade Hall

9. Clifton Suspension Bridge

10. 1880s

Answers to Politicians & Statesmen

1. Otto von Bismarck

2. Giuseppe Mazzini

3. Winston Churchill

4. Adolphe Thiers

5. James Buchanan

6. Eleven – although several of them had more than one term of office.

7. Henry Clay

8. John Alexander Macdonald

9. Duke of Wellington

10. Cecil Rhodes

Answers to Who Lived Here?

1. Benjamin Disraeli

2. William Wordsworth

3. The Churchills

4. Charles Dickens

5. Rothschild

6. The Brontes

7. Rupert Brooke

8. Alfred, Lord Tennyson

9. Emile Zola

10. Guernsey

Answers to Queen Victoria

1. Edward, Duke of Kent

2. First cousin

3. Nine

4. In what year was Queen Victoria created Empress of India?

5. King Charles spaniel

6. Kensington Palace

7. Osborne House

8. Grandmother

9. William Gladstone

10. Frogmore

Answers to Other Monarchs of the Victorian Era

1. Frederick III

2. Leopold I

3. Alfonso XIII

4. William I

5. Franz Josef of Austria

6. Louis Philippe

7. Nicholas I

8. Ludwig II

9. The hunting lodge at Mayerling

10. Ten

Answers to Tragedies and Accidents

1. Over a thousand people were crushed to death.

2. Tay Bridge disaster.

3. Johnstown

4. 1871

5. Potato

6. Princess Alice

7. Bubonic Plague

8. Winter Palace

9. The Great Blizzard

10. Sheffield

Answers to Business & Retail

1. Marks & Spencer

2. Haverhill, Massachusetts,

3. Fortnum and Mason

4. Maple & Co.

5. Harry Selfridge

6. Harrods

7. 1870s

8. Pennsylvania

9. Boots

10. House of Worth

Answers to Battles & Warfare

1. Austria & Prussia

2. Napoleon III

3. Balaclava

4. Gordon

5. Gettysburg

6. Greece & the Ottoman Empire

7. Zulu War

8. 1881

9. First Afghan War

10. Helmuth von Moltke

Answers to Scandals

1. The Dreyfus Case

2. Harriet Mordaunt

3. Tranby Croft

4. Cleveland Street

5. Effie (Euphemia) Gray

6. John Singer Sergeant

7. Branwell Bronte

8. Oscar Wilde

9. Grover Cleveland

10. Andrew Johnson

Answers to Reformers & Philanthropists

1. Elizabeth Fry

2. Florence Nightingale

3. Harriet Tubman

4. Josephine Butler

5. George Cadbury

6. William Booth

7. Octavia Hill

8. George Peabody

9. Earl of Shaftesbury

10. A campaigner for university education for women, and the first practising female physician in Scotland

Answers to Popular Songs

1. Dead

2. The Lost Chord

3. Monte Carlo

4. Gray

5. Maude

6. 'Come and buy my pretty flowers'

7. Love's Old Sweet Song

8. That wheel

9. A Life on the Ocean Wave

10. Mandalay

Answers to Sports, Games & Leisure

1. The Prince of Wales'

2. A juggling game

3. Wanderers

4. Queensbury

5. He was the first Men's Singles Wimbledon champion.

6. Maud Watson

7. Captain Webb

8. Bicycle

9. The modern Olympic Games

10. Circus

Answers to Medicine & Health

1. Joseph Lister

2. Louis Pasteur

3. Mary Seacole

4. St. Thomas'

5. A water pump

6. William Osler

7. Henry Gray

8. Elizabeth Garrett Anderson

9. She was a woman who disguised herself as a man in order to become an army doctor

10. Dr Thomas Neill Cream

Answers to Explorers

1. Richard Burton

2. William John Wills

3. Isabella Eberhardt

4. Henry Morton Stanley

5. Mary Kingsley

6. Edward John Eyre

7. Isabella Bird

8. Nellie Bly (Elizabeth Cochrane Seaman)

9. Alexandrine Tinné

10. William Hunter Workman

If you enjoyed these quizzes, you might also enjoy *The Alphabetical Quiz Book* by the same compiler.

Printed in Great Britain
by Amazon

41912547R00029